What Did You Really Say?

UNDERSTANDING THE DESTRUCTIVE EFFECTS OF PROFANITY

By

Alfonzo King Surrett, Jr.

Foreword by E.L. Warren

What Did You Really Say?
Understanding the Destructive Effects of Profanity

All Scripture references are from the Authorized King James Version of the Bible, unless otherwise marked.

References marked *"NAS"* are from the New American Standard Bible, copyright © 1960, 1962, 1963, 1968, 1971, 1972, 1973, 1977 by the Lockman Foundation, La Habra, California. All rights reserved.

References marked *"AMPLIFIED"* are from the Amplified Bible © copyright 1987 by the Zondervan Corporation and the Lockman Foundation, La Habra Foundation, California. All rights reserved.

Published by:

Ebed Publications
P.O. 3595
Hagerstown, MD 21742-3595

ISBN 1-884369-30-8

Printed in the United States of America

In Memory Of:

Mrs. Geraldine Lenora (Edwards) Surrett

Gerald Ogden Surrett

Mrs. Mabra (Hebert) Crowell

and

Mr. Harry Crowell

Dedication

I would like to dedicate this effort to my loving wife, Debra; my wonderful children, Gabrielle, Alfonzo III, Cara and Nicole; my brothers and sisters, Cassandra, Maleia, Clydonna, Clifford, Mark, and Steven; all of my nieces, nephews, uncles, aunts, and cousins and my precious in-laws.

ACKNOWLEDGMENTS

A special word of appreciation, gratitude and honor goes to my father, the Reverend A. K. Surrett, Sr., for the guidance, wisdom, direction and leadership he has imparted to my life.

Special thanks to Lisa Mitchell: Lisa, thank you for your long trips from the far North Side to the South Suburbs and the many hours of typing. You are truly a blessing. Anyone who can read my handwriting is truly anointed (smile). You will forever be a member of the Surrett Family. We love you (Cee-Sa).

Special thanks to Henrietta Mason: Henrietta, first I am grateful to Archie, Prentice, Armenta, Elizabeth, Jonathan and Rachel for allowing you to give so much time to this project. Your time, talent, suggestions, hard work and prayers are greatly appreciated. Thank you for your belief in and support of my vision.

Contents

Foreword

Rarely does a book come along that addresses matters that affect both believers and unbelievers with an approach that doesn't alienate either. ***What Did You Really Say?*** is just such a book. It is a must for use in the school systems, the correctional institutions, and youth ministries. And every adult should read it, as well.

This book arms the reader with knowledge and wisdom about the power of words and their ability to create life or destroy it. It takes a clear look at a dirty subject and leaves you feeling fresh and equipped to assist others in leaving the gutters of profanity for the streets of prosperity.

Our Creator only wants what is good and excellent for all that He created. I pray that as you read this book you will be lifted to a new level of communication in your quest to be all that God called you to be.

E. L. Warren
Pastor, Cathedral of Worship, Quincy, Illinois
President, E. L. Warren Ministries International

Introduction

I have noticed, as I'm sure you have, an increase in the use of profanity in our society. We have become so accustomed to its use, in fact, that it seems as if we have accepted such language as normal. I remember a time, however, when profanity was considered to be the language of the uneducated, the brutish, and of some few adult males. Now profanity can be heard rolling off of the tongues of highly educated people, even of successful, respected, and well groomed women.

As I was growing up, children would never dare to use dirty words, especially in public; and those who did dare to cuss in private made sure that no adult could hear them and that no one told on them. How times have changed!

Today you may hear adults, teenagers, and even children using some of the most vulgar language imaginable in front of a group of ladies, senior citizens, ministers or anyone else for that matter — and think nothing of it. They will even dare you to say something about it. Many children and young people have bought into the lie that profanity makes you feel or sound more like a real man, more grown-up. They are deceived.

The proliferation of profanity in our modern society has had a negative effect on our homes and schools, on our jobs, on entertainment and sports, on the media, and on many other areas of our lives. Why has this matter gotten so out of hand? It takes a responsible individual to realize the negative effects of profanity and to make a constructive decision to refuse to use any such form of destructive communication.

Let me be the first to confess that I have been guilty in the past of using every profane, vulgar, and destructive word imaginable; and nothing in this book is intended to put down anyone who may still be using such language.

I have confessed my sin to my Lord and Savior Jesus Christ, and He has forgiven me; and He will do the same for anyone else who is willing to recognize their wrong. His Word declares:

> *If we confess our sins He is faithful and just to forgive us of our sins, and to cleanse us from all unrighteousness.* 1 John 1:9

The Prophet Isaiah had a personal encounter with God. He found himself in the holy presence of the Lord, and in the beautiful light of God's glory, his sin was revealed. In confession, he wrote:

> *Then said I, Woe [ruined or dead] is me! For I am undone [destroyed], because I am a man of unclean lips, and I dwell in the midst of a people of unclean lips: for mine eyes have seen the King, the Lord of hosts.* Isaiah 6:5

Just then something wonderful happened. God had a remedy for the prophet's failure. One of Heaven's creatures was sent to take a live coal from the altar of God and place it upon the prophet's lips, purging him of his sin and sealing his lips for constructive use:

> *Then flew one of the seraphims [heavenly beings] unto me, having a live coal in his hand, which he had taken with the tongs from off the altar: And he laid it upon my mouth, and said, Lo [behold], this has touched thy lips; and your iniquity [sin] is taken away, and your sin is purged [completely forgiven].* Isaiah 6:6-7

I thank God for doing that same miracle in my own life; and I hope, through writing this book, to be instrumental in bringing deliverance to many others who find themselves bound by this insidious evil of cursing. My war is not against those who use profanity, but against the spirit of profanity itself. When that spirit is recognized and its power broken through Jesus Christ, any man, woman, boy or girl may be set free from a filthy tongue.

I believe that:

If we change the way we think,
We will change what we say;
If we change what we say,
We will change what we do;
And if we change what we do,
We will change our world.

It's time to make that change!

May the Spirit of the Lord bless you as you read ***What Did You Really Say?***

Your Brother,
Alfonzo King Surrett Jr.

Part I

Understanding Profanity

- 1 -

What's In A Word?

So shall my word be that goeth forth out of my mouth: it shall not return unto me void, but it shall accomplish that which I please, and it shall prosper in the thing whereto I sent it.

Isaiah 55:11

A *word* is *a unit of language consisting of one or more spoken sounds, or their written representation, that functions as a principal carrier of meaning.* It is *a verbal or written expression of thought.*

As human beings, we were made in the image of God to communicate with both God and man, primarily through the use of words. Even those who cannot speak or hear communicate by writing words or by using sign language, and in sign language, each sign represents a word, or letters that make up a word.

Words then are the primary tool through which we are able to express our feelings, desires, beliefs, needs, and thoughts to others.

Words are very powerful, for good or for evil. They can instruct, inform and inspire, or they can insult, inflame and injure. It all depends on the motive of the person who is speaking and the way in which the words are spoken.

The old saying *"sticks and stones can break my bones, but words will never hurt me"* couldn't be further from the truth. Words can hurt and do hurt, and they can and do heal. Words bring life, and words bring death. Words inspire peace and words incite war. Words are the most powerful weapon we have at our disposal. To use them carelessly is like putting a nuclear weapon into the hands of an unruly child.

Words are seeds. They produce their own kind. Take, for example, the planting of an apple seed. A tiny apple seed has the power to produce a whole tree with hundreds of apples on it. Each apple has within it several seeds, and each of these seeds has the same ability to produce and multiply. Therefore, one seed has the potential of producing an entire orchard, each tree of which has the potential to produce more and more apples, and each of those apple contains more seeds. The process thus continues over and over again.

The very same is true with words. When you speak a word, you are planting it. Whether you speak words of life, love, peace, joy and blessings, or words of profanity or cursing, you will reap what you sow.

The Bible says:

> *While the earth remains, seedtime and harvest,*

> *and cold and heat, and summer and winter, and day and night shall not cease.*
>
> Genesis 8:22 NAS

This is the law of seedtime and harvest, one of God's unchanging laws. What you sow you reap.

We owe it to ourselves and others to learn more about the purpose and function of words and to begin to use them properly. In doing so we will see that much of the negativity that we have experienced has been brought upon us by our own misuse and abuse of words. We will also realize that we can change our circumstances by making the decision to use creative words: the words of God, our Creator.

The first rule about words we must learn is that our words must never contradict the Word of God. We must have faith in His Word, faith that comes by hearing it, and our faith will produce fruit in us. Jesus said:

> *If ye abide in me, and my words abide in you, ye shall ask what ye will, and it shall be done unto you.*
>
> John 15:7

The Bible was originally written in Hebrew and Greek. In the Greek, two of the words that have been translated *word* are *Rhema* and *Logos*. *Rhema* denotes *that which is spoken, what is uttered in speech or writing. Rhema* stands for *the subject matter of the word; the thing spoken about. Rhema* is *the operative or all powerful word or command of God.*

Logos denotes *intelligence* and is *the expression of that intelligence*. Logos is not the mere name of an object; It is *that which has within it a concept or idea.*

Logos is used in the Bible to describe *a word from God the Father, or Jesus Christ. Logos* is *the revealed will of God; a message from the Lord our Creator, delivered with his authority and made effective by His power.*

Jesus Christ, in His pre-incarnate state, is called, in the Bible, *Logos,* or *The Word:*

> *In the beginning was the Word, and the Word was with God, and the Word was God.*
>
> John 1:1

Logos, The Word, the personal manifestation of God in Christ, the expression and the communication of The Word of God to man:

> *For in Him Jesus Christ dwelleth all the fullness of the Godhead bodily.* Colossians 2:9

Jesus is the embodiment of The Word of God:

> *And The Word was made flesh, and dwelt among us.* John 1:14

God's Word, then, is His expression of Himself:

God is *Omnipotent* which means *all powerful.*

God is *Omnipresent* which means He is *present in all places, at all times.*

God is *Omniscient* which means He is *all knowledge, all wisdom and all understanding.*

Jesus Christ is the expression of God's power, wisdom, knowledge, and presence in the earth. And He is the Originator of all things:

> *In the beginning was The Word [Logos], and The Word was with God, and The Word was God. The same was in the beginning with God. All things were made by Him; and without Him was not anything made that was made. In Him was life; and the life was the light of men.*
>
> John 1:1-4

So *The Word* existed before creation. In fact, all of creation was brought into being by *The Word:* the whole universe, the sun, moon, and stars, the planets and galaxies, plants, animals, and even mankind. Everything was created by *The Word,* and without *The Word* nothing was created.

In the Genesis account of the Creation, two phrases are repeated over and over. They are *"and God said"* and *"and it was so."* This tells us how God created the whole universe. He spoke it into existence. The universe was created by the Word of God. God, expressing himself by His Word, brought the universe from the Divine intellect into material existence:

Divine Intelligence (*omniscience*) thought it.

The Word (*omnipotence*) formed it.

The Spirit (*omnipresence*) revealed it.

God's Word is powerful and effective. The prophet Isaiah foretold that God's Word would never fail to accomplish its purpose:

> *So shall my word be that goeth forth out of my mouth: it shall not return unto me void, but it shall accomplish that which I please, and it shall prosper in the thing whereto I sent it.*
>
> Isaiah 55:11

The writer of Hebrews revealed that God holds the world up *"by the word of His power"*:

> *God, who at sundry times and in divers manners SPOKE in time past unto the fathers by the prophets, has in these last days SPOKEN unto us by his Son, who He has appointed heir of all things, by whom also He made the worlds; who being the brightness of His glory, and the express image of His person and upholding all things* BY THE WORD OF HIS POWER, *when He had by himself purged our sins, sat down on the right hand of the majesty on high; Being made so much better than the angels, as He has by inheritance obtained a more excellent name than they.* Hebrews 1:1-3

In all of this, God has shown us the unique importance of words, and their power in our lives. Words are powerful, for good or for evil. A compliment can lift a person up, while an insult can bring a person down. A word of encouragement can inspire a person to continue despite the difficulty of the task, while a word of discouragement can cause a person to quit, no matter how easy the task at hand may be. And the spirit from which we speak determines the end result.

I believe that much of the negativity that we see in society and in our personal lives is a direct result of the words we speak.

What's in a word? That's a loaded question.

- 2 -

What's In A Name?

And she shall bring forth a son, and thou shalt call his name JESUS: for he shall save his people from their sins. Now all this was done, that it might be fulfilled which was spoken of the Lord by the prophet, saying, Behold, a virgin shall be with child, and shall bring forth a son, and they shall call his name Emmanuel, which being interpreted is, God with us. Matthew 1:21-23

A *name* is *a word or group of words by which a person, place, thing, group of people, organization or idea is known or recognized.*

In Bible times, a person's name usually had a specific meaning and was an indication of that person's character or a particular quality which he or she exemplified. Below are just a few examples of the many instances of this in sacred Scripture:

Abraham	*Father of a multitude*

(He is the father of both Arab and Jewish nations.)

Moses	*Drawn out*

(He was drawn out of the Nile River by Pharaoh's daughter; and he was drawn out of Egypt by the mighty hand of God.)

Jesus	*God who is salvation*
Josiah	*Jehovah heads*
Jacob	*Heel catcher, supplanter*
David	*Beloved*

As we can see, each of these names describes something of the character, personality or life of the individual. So names are important.

God also has a name, but since a single name could never fully describe all that God is, the Bible uses many names for Him.

> *In the beginning God created the heaven and the earth.* Genesis 1:1

In this verse, the Hebrew word translated *God* is *Elohim*. It is a compound word. *El* means *mighty, strong, prominent, sovereign. Im* is a plural ending in Hebrew, showing the manifestation of God as three persons, the Trinity or Tri-Unity of God: Father, Son, and Holy Spirit. Still He is one God, *Elohim.*

Another of God's names is *Jehovah,* which means *The Ever Revealing One*. God reveals Himself in many compound names using *Jehovah* as the base:

Jehovah Jireh	*The Lord our Provider*
Jehovah Rophe	*The Lord our Healing*
Jehovah Shalom	*The Lord our Peace*
Jehovah Rohi	*The Lord our Shepherd*
Jehovah Shammah	*The Lord is There*

Others of God's names are:

El Shaddai	*God Almighty (more than enough)*
El Elyon	*God Most High*
Adonai	*Master, Owner*

Each of God's many names is important as it reveals something new to us about Who He is.

Names have a significance. So, when we call people dirty names, we are ascribing to them dirty characteristics. And when you use the Holy names of God in vain, it is a very serious act, for which He will not hold you guiltless.

What's in a name? Plenty!

- 3 -

The Gift of Speech and Its Abuse

And God said, Let us make man in our image, according to our likeness. Genesis 1:26

The Hebrew word for *image* is *Tselem* which means: *to shade; not the exact duplicate, a representative of the original, lacking the essential character of the original.*

God made man in His *image*. In order to have a physical representation of Himself in the earth, He formed man from the dust of the ground. God made man to be the *shadow* or *reflection* of His character, knowledge, righteousness, and holiness. He wanted man to be the fruit, or offspring, of His Spirit and destined man to express this fruit in the world:

The fruit of the Spirit is love, joy, peace, longsuffering, gentleness, goodness, faith, meekness, temperance: against such there is no law.
Galatians 5:22-23

The Hebrew word for *likeness* is *damah* which means *to compare, to resemble, liken, be like.* Man was created in the *image* and according to the *likeness* of God. Therefore man, like no other creature on earth, has the ability to use words to express himself. Some might say, "Even a parrot can speak," but the truth of the matter is that a parrot can only mimic speech.

The word *mimic* means *to imitate.* A parrot only imitates the sound that it has heard from someone or something else. A parrot does not have the ability to express its own thoughts. It does not have the ability to speak based upon its own understanding. The ability to communicate through speech is reserved only for man.

To speak is *to convey thoughts through the use of words, to communicate verbally one's own thoughts.* Of all God's creation only man, being like God, has the power to express his intellect as he wills through the thoughtful use of words – either written or spoken. Speech is a gift to mankind from a loving God.

The ability to speak plays an important role in man's relationship and fellowship with God. For example, there is no salvation apart from man's ability to express himself in words:

> *If thou shalt confess with thy mouth the Lord Jesus, and shalt believe in thine heart that God hath raised him from the dead, thou shalt be saved.* Romans 10:9

There is no forgiveness apart from man's ability to

express himself in words:

> *If we confess our sins, He is faithful and just to forgive us our sins, and to cleanse us from all unrighteousness.* 1 John 1:9

There could be no answers to prayer apart from man's ability to express himself in words:

> *And all things, whatsoever you shall ask in prayer, believing, you shall receive.*
> Matthew 21:22

All of the things we do in the church, as part of the maintenance of our ongoing relationship with God and our fellow believers (worship, witnessing, preaching, prophesying, teaching, etc.), depend on our ability to speak.

And if our words have the power to be an effective force in our relationship with God, our Creator, then they also have the power to be an effective force in our relationship with all that He has created.

Since speech is a gift from God, our ability to speak should work in agreement with His Word, resulting in blessing for all those around us. When our speech results in cursing we have violated the purpose of God in granting us this precious gift.

Profanity, then, is an abuse of the privilege of communication. This is the reason God has said:

> *For by thy words thou shall be justified, and by*

thy words thou shall be condemned.

Matthew 12:34-37

What exactly is profanity? *Profanity* is *the lack of reverence toward God or sacred things.* Something that is *profane* is *unholy, heathen, pagan, or vulgar.*

Profanity is *vulgar language.* The word *vulgar* means *the ignorance of or lack of good breeding or taste; unrefined; crude; indecent; obscene; lewd.*

The word *curse* is *the expression of a wish that misfortune, evil, or death come upon someone; a profane oath; an evil that has been invoked upon a person; the cause of evil, misfortune, or trouble; to blaspheme; to speak curses; swear profanely.*

Through profanity, therefore, Satan turns the gift of God against its Creator; and, if we cooperate with him, we set ourselves as enemies of God and His plan for our lives. This is serious business. Speech is a gift from God that we must not be guilty of misusing.

- 4 -

How Words Affect Us

For my thoughts are not your thoughts, neither are your ways my ways, saith the Lord. For as the heavens are higher than the earth, so are my ways higher than your ways, and my thoughts than your thoughts. Isaiah 55:8-9

To appreciate the power of words and their potential effect on our lives, we need to see ourselves as God sees us. God, who is a Triune Being (Father, Son, and Holy Spirit), created man to be a triune being (spirit, soul, and body). Man is a spirit; he has a soul, and he lives in a body. The soul is the mind, the will and the emotions and includes the imagination and memory. It is the link between the body and the spirit. Words affect every part of our being.

Words Affect the Spirit

God created man in His image and according to

His likeness because He wanted to have fellowship with us. The Greek word for *fellowship* is *koinonia,* which means *communion, fellowship, sharing in common and communication*. It is through the spirit that we have fellowship or communion with God.

> *God is a Spirit: and they that worship Him must worship him in spirit and in truth.* John 4:24

True worship is communion, communication and having fellowship with God in the spirit. Satan seeks, through the use of improper words, to damage our spirits so that we cannot properly communicate with God. When the spirit is damaged, our relationship with God is damaged as well, and our fellowship with Him is lessened or cut off.

Words Affect the Mind

The *mind* is *the agency or part of man that reasons, understands or perceives, the center of all mental activity.* This mental activity produces thoughts, which we express, primarily through words and actions. The mind controls the body and the bodily functions. The body responds and reacts based upon the information and instructions given to it by the mind.

As a result of being made in the image and according to the likeness of God, man, like God, has intelligence. In other words, man has the capacity for reasoning, for understanding, for knowledge and wisdom, for the gathering and distribution of information. Man, through his God-given mind, also has the power to make intelligent choices.

Man, like God, his Creator, has the power to communicate his thoughts, desires, opinions, feelings, beliefs, fears, intentions, needs, etc. through words. Words, therefore, are an expression of the mind. Satan attempts to place evil thoughts in our minds through the wrong use of words. He wants to confuse our minds, and to cause our thoughts to be diverted away from God. Words leave a strong impression on the mind and affect how we think and how we speak.

Words Affect the Will

The *will* is *the power of control that the mind has over its own actions;* the will is *your ability to choose your thoughts, words, and actions.* Your will is *your desire.*

God, in His infinite wisdom, created man with a free will, giving us the power to make decisions for ourselves. He did this so that we could choose to love and serve Him. However, with the first man and woman, it didn't work out that way. In the Garden of Eden, Adam and Eve had the power to choose whose words they would obey: the word of God, the Creator, or the word of Satan, the destroyer. Sadly, they made a wrong choice.

> *Now the serpent was more subtle [cunning] than any beast of the field which the Lord God*

> *had made. And he said unto the woman, "Yea, hath God said ... ?"* Genesis 3:1

Satan knew that man was created by the word of God and that man's source of life is the same word of God. Therefore, the only way he would be able to destroy man would be to separate him from the word of God. Satan was not more powerful than man, and he did not have the authority to take life from man, but he was cunning, and he persuaded Adam and Eve to disobey God. Through this one act, man relinquished his authority and power over Satan.

God had warned Adam what would happen if he disobeyed:

> *In the day that you eat thereof you shall surely die.* Genesis 2:17

But Satan assured Adam that what God had said was not true. Satan said:

> *You shall not surely die.* Genesis 3:4

The result of man's willingness to believe and obey the word of Satan, and his unwillingness to believe and obey the word of God was just as God had said:

> *The wages [payment] of sin is death; but the gift of God is eternal life through Jesus Christ our Lord.* Romans 6:23

In the same way that he influenced Adam and Eve to make an improper decision, Satan seeks to influence the will of each one of us and to lure us to his side. We each have the power to choose who we will obey and the power to choose whose words we will speak.

Words Affect the Emotions

Emotion is *the sensitive area of consciousness in which love, joy, sorrow, fear, hate and other feelings are experienced.* Usually these feelings are accompanied by certain physical changes, such as increased heartbeat, heavy breathing, or loss of breath, crying, laughing, shaking, perspiration, etc.

Emotional responses are too often based on what we perceive to be true as opposed to what is actually true. Unfortunately, feelings can be deceptive and may change at any given moment. Likewise, perceptions can be true or false. Our emotions alone cannot tell the difference.

Satan seeks to influence our emotions so that he can control our actions and our words. Often when we are emotionally upset, that is the time that we speak words that we don't really mean. Our emotions overpower our better judgement; and, too often, this brings negative results into our lives and the lives of others.

Words can be used to express emotions, and words can cause an emotional reaction in the hearer. A person whose actions and words are based on emotion alone is a very unstable person. The emotions need the help of the mind, which processes the information, analyzes it and decides its importance and what the proper response should be. Emotional response without reason brings chaos. Words spoken from emotions alone can be very dangerous and bring much confusion, and result in contradictions and the need for many apologies.

Through his lies and deceit, Satan seeks to confuse us and cause us to make emotional responses that will cost us dearly later.

Words affect every area of our lives, and what we say affects others in the very same way.

- 5 -

The Origins of Profanity

Words originated in the heavenlies, as we have seen, and God is their source. Then where did profanity originate? God certainly didn't create it, and it certainly didn't originate with the holy angels. Of them the Bible teaches:

> *They are all ministering spirits, sent forth to minister for them who are heirs of salvation.*
>
> Hebrews 1:14

> *Bless the Lord, ye his angels, that excel in strength, that do his commandments, hearkening unto the voice of His word.*
>
> Psalms 103:20

Angels are creatures of blessing. They are *"sent forth to minister"* to those who love God. Angels are respectful and obedient beings. They do God's commandments. They hearken to His voice.

So profanity originated with Satan, that archenemy of God and of God's people, who took God's gift of words and profaned it. The Bible teaches us that Satan, who is, in reality, a fallen angel, has three goals – *"to steal, to kill, and to destroy":*

> *The thief cometh not, but for to steal, and to kill, and to destroy: I am come that they might have life, and that they might have it more abundantly.* John 10:10

Satan is profane and delights in profaning the things of God and the spirit and mind of man, the crowning glory of God's creation. By causing man to blaspheme and curse God and man, Satan feels that he is hurting God and dragging down what God loves most, the soul of man.

And just as there are holy angels who do God's bidding and hearken to His voice, there are unholy or fallen angels, also known as demons, who do the will of Satan and hearken to his voice. These are demons of filth, sent forth to pollute the earth.

If the holy angels bring blessings, the unholy angels (demons) bring curses. If the holy angels do God's commandments, the unholy angels do Satan's commandments. If the holy angels hearken unto (obey) the voice of God, the unholy angels hearken unto (obey) the voice of Satan.

When we give our voice to speak positively, words that please God and bless men, God's mighty angels are set to work to bring our word to pass, just as if God had spoken it himself.

Unfortunately, the same is true in the negative. When we speak negatively, when we gossip, lie or use profanity, we are granting permission to or actually instructing demon spirits to carry out the words that we speak. When curses are uttered, demons respond with glee and attempt to bring the thing to pass which has been spoken.

Spirits usually need a body in order to function or operate in the physical or material world. God, who is a spirit, came in a flesh or physical body in order to rescue dying humanity. He came as The Word.

Satan and his legions of demons also desire a flesh body through which they can operate in the earth. When we use vulgar language, gossip or lie, when we deceive ourselves and others, we give Satan and his cohorts permission to work through our bodies, bodies which were created to be the temple of the Holy Spirit.

Since we have voices and have been created with a free will to choose whose words we will speak, Satan and his demons constantly seek to corrupt us and make us their slaves. At the same time, the Spirit of God woos us to Himself, desiring to use our abilities as a blessing.

We thus have the opportunity of becoming either representatives of God or of Satan. When we give voice to someone else's opinions, feelings or beliefs, we are speaking in their behalf, and we become their representatives. When we use profanity or curse, we are willingly allowing the spirit of Satan to use our tongue; and we, in essence, become his representatives.

When God created us in His image and according to His likeness, He intended us to be *His* representatives in the earth. We were created to speak words that bless, not words that curse.

Many justify themselves, saying that they only use profanity occasionally or that they never mean to hurt anyone. But that is like pulling the trigger of a gun and later saying that you didn't mean to kill anybody. The bullet is just as deadly, whether the intent was to kill or not. And curse words are just as deadly as bullets. We need to think before we speak.

Most people use profanity because they heard someone else use it. Children, for example, usually begin because they hear it from someone older than themselves: a parent or an older brother or sister. And most people have never given much thought to the meaning or origin of the words they speak.

But words are created by spirit, and they reveal and give life to the motives and intents of the spirit from which they originate. This is what we mean when we say that we have been "inspired" by someone's words. Their words have given new life to us concerning a particular matter.

The word *inspire* has two parts to it: *in,* meaning *inside,* and *spire,* meaning *spirit, or to breathe.* We have life through Divine inspiration:

> *And the Lord God formed man of the dust of the ground, and breathed into [inspired] his nostrils the breath [spirit] of life; and man became a living soul.* Genesis 2:7

The opposite of inspire is expire. *Ex* meaning *out,* and *spire* meaning *spirit.* Therefore when someone expires, the spirit or life is expelled from them and they die. There are many spirits in the world, and they either come from God, who is the Holy Spirit, the Spirit of life, or they come from Satan, the unholy spirit, the spirit of death.

In the same way, every word that is spoken either originates from God the Spirit of Life, or from Satan the Spirit of death. All profanity originates with Satan and his evil purposes, and nothing good can come of it.

Part II

Specific Curses and Their Effects

- 6 -

DAMNING SOMEONE

> *And God blessed them, And God said unto them, Be fruitful, and multiply, and replenish [fill] the earth, and subdue it: and have dominion over the fish of the sea, and over the fowl of the air, and over every living thing that moves upon the earth.* Genesis 1:28

The worst thing about the curses used to damn someone is that we include God, as if He were doing the damning. But God is a God of blessing, not a God of cursing. His blessings have always been with those who trust Him and obey His commands. But He doesn't even damn His enemies.

Those who choose not to obey God's commandments forfeit His blessings and give themselves over to Satan, becoming the objects of his curses and damnations. It is never God who curses or damns a person. If they are cursed, it is by an act of their own will, and because they have chosen to disobey and turn away from God.

When we are in obedience to the Word of God and speak according to His will, we invoke His blessings, and His power is available to us. But when we choose to disobey God's Word and speak against His will, we deliberately move ourselves away from His blessings. It is only then that Satan's power, his curse and his damnation, become operative in our lives.

God does not damn! Satan damns!
God does not curse! Satan curses!

God is a God of blessing. Damnation and curses can come upon us only when we allow Satan to have access to our affairs, when we open to him our thinking and our speech. God would never curse us. In fact, He goes to unfathomable extremes to bless us, often when we are not worthy of those blessings.

In the Genesis account, we see how God, by the Word, created the heavens and the earth. He created light: the sun, moon, stars, planets, and galaxies; the air we breathe; the magnificent oceans, rivers, waterfalls, and streams; the vegetation: trees, plants, beautiful flowers; animals: cattle and wild beasts of the field, fish and birds of all kinds. This was all a blessing that He expressly created for man's pleasure. He blessed man with woman, and woman with man. He blessed man and woman with children, all for our pleasure.

God blessed mankind with the ability to give and receive love. He blessed us with the privilege to fellowship and commune with Him, as Father, Son and

Holy Spirit. And God has blessed us with angels to protect and minister to us.

All of this was a manifestation of His love and concern for mankind; for after God had prepared the earth for man's habitation, He created man in His image, and according to His likeness, both male and female. And when man arrived, the first thing God did was to bless him:

> *And God blessed them, And God said unto them, Be fruitful, and multiply, and replenish [fill] the earth, and subdue it: and have dominion over the fish of the sea, and over the fowl of the air, and over every living thing that moves upon the earth.* Genesis 1:28

God blessed man and gave him authority over all that He had created. He blessed man with the privilege of having a personal relationship with His Creator. We serve a God of blessing!

Because of His love for mankind, God warned Adam and Eve not to eat from the tree of the knowledge of good and evil. He could eat from every other tree except that one:

> *And the Lord God commanded the man, saying, of every tree of the garden you may freely eat: but of the tree of the knowledge of good and evil, you shall not eat of it: for in the day that you eat of it you shall surely die.* Genesis 2:16-17

God never cursed man. The curse came as a result of man's choosing to turn away from the blessed Word of God and its benefits. When man willingly chose to obey the word of Satan, the result was sickness, pain, disappointment, and death.

God, of course, knew man's choice from the beginning, but His love compelled Him to give mankind a chance. And, when He knew that man would choose against him and fall, God still did not curse him. Instead He created a plan of salvation whereby we could be redeemed, forgiven, and saved. From the foundations of the world, it was determined that the Lamb of God, God's only Son, Jesus Christ, would come to earth to pay the awesome price for our salvation. All of this was a manifestation of God's love and blessing for mankind:

> *For God so loved the world, that He gave His only begotten son, that whosoever believes in Him shall not perish, but have everlasting life.*
>
> John 3:16

When we say, therefore, that God damned anyone or anything, we are blaming God for the works of Satan. And when we command God to damn anyone or anything, we are acting as if God could go against all that He is, to become all that Satan is. God will never do that! To say the least, it is foolish to trifle with the Creator of the universe by using such profane language. And to say that God damns is the ultimate lie. He never has, and He never will!

- 7 -

Cursing Women

> *And God saw everything that He had made, and behold, it was very good.* Genesis 1:31

As God finished the various aspects of creation, He stepped back to observe His handiwork; and, in every case, decided that it was *"good."* The phrase *"And God saw that it was good"* is repeated over and over in the first chapter of Genesis.

Man was the culmination, the crowning glory of God's creation. Placing man in the midst of all the rest of creation suddenly made sense of it all. So, when God had finished creating man, His observation changed somewhat. Now God's handiwork was no longer just *"good"*; it was *"very good."*

Each of the animals had its mate, for God created them male and female. Each species had the amazing ability to reproduce offspring of its own kind. Furthermore, all the animals lived in harmony, relating easily and naturally with one another.

But, although God had given Adam authority over

all the earth and its myriad creatures, and although Adam had the privilege of naming all the animals, he did not have anyone with whom he could relate personally. He was not like any of the other animals. He was a unique creation. He needed a mate, for fellowship and for procreation of the human race. He was alone and lonely.

> *And the Lord God said, It is not good that the man should be alone; I will make him an help meet for him.* Genesis 2:18

This was the first time, since the amazing process of creation had begun, that God said anything was *"not good."* Everything, up to this point, had been either *"good"* or *"very good."* What was *"not good"*? It was *"not good"* that Adam was alone. There was much that he could not do on his own. He needed a mate.

Woman, then, was the answer to man's need. She was the completion of his person. She made up the lack and provided what Adam could not provide. She did for him what he could not do for himself.

She was not complete either, as Eve quickly learned, I am sure. She needed Adam. He was her other, necessary part, and the two of them together made a whole.

Now, Adam was no longer alone. He had not been able to converse with the lions or the fish or the sparrows, but he could communicate to his heart's content with the woman God had given him.

Woman, then, was a very special gift of God for man, and since God wanted it to be a surprise, he put Adam to sleep:

> *And the Lord God caused a deep sleep to fall upon Adam, and he slept: and he took one of his ribs, and closed up the flesh instead thereof; and the rib, which the Lord God had taken from man, made he a woman, and brought her unto the man.* Genesis 2: 21-25

Can't you just see it? — a loving father presenting a perfect bride to his beloved son. What a wonderful God we serve! This was the first marriage, and the institution of Holy Matrimony.

Adam was pleased:

> *And Adam said, This is now bone of my bone and flesh of my flesh: she shall be called woman, because she was taken out of man. Therefore shall a man leave his father and his mother, and shall cleave unto his wife: and they shall be one flesh. And they were both naked, the man and his wife, and were not ashamed.* Genesis 2:23

A woman is something very special. She is the expression of our Father's love, the proof that God knows and understands our every thought and need and wants to replace our loneliness and suffering in this present world with joy, and beauty, and love. Woman is a precious gift from God.

Other biblical writers agree:

> *Whoever finds a wife finds a good thing, and obtains favor of the Lord.* Proverbs 18:22

Woman: Her beauty surpasses that of all the stars and galaxies. Her smell is more lovely than that of a field of flowers. Her touch is more soothing than that of a soft, summer breeze. The sound of her voice is far more glorious than the singing of tiny birds at dawn. And her taste is sweeter than the taste of honey from the honeycomb.

Why then are so many curses directed at women?

It is not surprising, for women have been under attack by Satan from the very beginning. Because they are a special creation of God, God's gift to earth, Satan hates women and will do anything in his power to degrade and drag them down.

It was Eve who was first attacked by Satan in the Garden. Adam was guilty of not preventing that attack. He could have done more to be aware of what was happening and to come to the aid of his woman. He had been given by God, after all, responsibility over all of creation. And ever since then it has been man's responsibility, in all decent and God-fearing societies, to protect women.

One of the problems regarding lack of respect for women is that few have recognized the power of women to influence our society. Too often she has been treated like a toy, to use and cast aside. But women exert a strong influence, over their husbands, over their children, and over their neighborhood – for good or for bad.

Men as strong as Samson have learned this lesson the hard way. He lost his source of strength in the process. Men as wise as Solomon have had to learn this lesson the hard way. He was intoxicated by the foolishness of strange women in his old age.

When Satan attacked God's special creation and had convinced her to eat of the forbidden fruit, it was not difficult for her to get Adam to agree, although they had both been warned by God not to do it.

There was a penalty for all concerned. The penalty pronounced over the serpent (Satan) helps us to understand his hatred of women and his campaign against them:

> *And the Lord God said to the serpent, "Because you have done this, you are cursed above all [domestic] animals and above every [wild] living thing of the field; upon your belly you shall go, and you shall eat dust [and what it contains] all the days of your life.*
> *"And I will put enmity between you and the woman, and between your offspring and her Offspring; He will bruise and tread your head underfoot, and you will lie in wait and bruise His heel."* Genesis 3:14-15 AMPLIFIED

The word *enmity* here means *a feeling or condition of hostility; hatred; ill will; animosity; antagonism.* This explains a lot of things. It should come as no surprise that much of the profanity used today consists of curses originating from the spirit of Satan against women.

There is a word for *the hatred of women*. It is *misogyny*. This word has two parts: *miso* which means *hatred,* and *gyny* which means *female or woman.* From *gyny* we get the word *gynecology,* which is *the branch of medical science that deals with the care of women with reference to reproduction and the reproductive organs.* A *gynecologist* is *a physician who specializes in treating women* and is sometimes called a *gyne.*

Misogyny is nothing new. It originated with Satan in the beginning of time. He hates women.

When we love women and respect them for the gift of God they are to our society and for the strong influence they can exercise over the affairs of men, we will never curse them or use any words that denigrate them in any way. On the contrary, we will bless them in word and deed.

Why is it that many curses are against mothers? The very name of the first woman created by God gives us a clue:

> *And Adam called his wife's name Eve; because she was the mother of all living.* Genesis 3:20

The woman God placed on the earth was to be the *"mother of all living."* Mothers are life-givers. Mothers are nurturers. So, when we use curses against mothers, we are speaking about the most sacred individual in the family. Aside from Jesus, there has never been a more important person alive in the earth than a mother. Without a mother, none of us would be here. God has blessed mothers with the gift of life. When we curse a mother, we are cursing all that she has the potential to produce and nurture to maturity.

God placed, in woman, a womb, a life-forming chamber where the souls of men could be united with their predetermined bodies, so that they could dwell on this earth. Barren wombs are not the will of God. Barrenness has always been considered a curse, and God doesn't curse. He blesses.

Yet many people take the term *mother* and attach it to the most filthy, vulgar, and profane word in the human vocabulary. It is the most degrading word you could ever speak, or wish upon anyone — male or female. The word denotes lust, rape, violation, filth, abomination, impurity, disrespect, hate, abuse and even murder. And this curse is spoken often enough in our present society that probably everyone reading these words has heard it — many times over.

How can people take such a vile curse and attach it to mother, the most precious person God ever created, woman, *"the mother of all living."*

Could there be a connection between the curses commonly spoken against women and mothers and the flood of rape, incest, and abuse of women currently being witnessed in our society? I am sure of it.

When we "play the dozens," talk negatively about each other's mother, jokingly or not, we are treading on dangerous territory. One of God's most basic commands is respect for our parents. And it is the only command with a promise attached to it:

> *Honor thy father and thy mother : That thy days may be long upon the land which the Lord thy God giveth thee.* Exodus 20:12

Could there be a connection between the way we dishonor our parents with curses and the number of young people who are dying every day from drugs, alcohol, aids, suicide and homicide? I am sure of it.

Another of the degrading terms used against a woman originally meant *a female dog*. Somewhere along the line it began to be used to denote *a bad or bad tempered women,* but eventually became *a strong term of contempt or hostility.* In simple words, it is an insult — of the strongest type.

In the Bible, a *dog* was considered unclean, and the term *dog* was used to describe heathen people, unbelievers. This seems to have little to do with the common use of the word today. Whatever the case, it is a serious sin to call someone who was created in the image and according to the likeness of God *a dog,* and it is also a serious sin to call someone the son of one, implying that their mother is a dog.

God cannot hold us guiltless when we use these curses, however popular they might be.

- 8 -

DEGRADING LOVE

And we have known and believed the love that God hath to us. God is love; and he that dwelleth in love dwelleth in God, and God in him.

1 John 4:16

We all believe that old saying that "What the world needs now is love." One of the most frequently used curse words, however, is a word that profanely refers to sexual intercourse, and degrades the act — in the crudest of terms.

Sexual intercourse is the most intimate form of communication; and God has shown His respect for this sacred act by commanding that it be shared only between a husband and his wife. It was created by God for their enjoyment, to bring them together as one in a loving relationship, and to produce the most blessed, precious gift that anyone can give or receive: a new life, children.

The sex act is to be enjoyed and shared between two people, a man and a woman, whom God has joined in Holy Matrimony. In this context, making love is the most personal, private, powerful, caring, giving and exciting experience that two people can share.

Why has God, our Creator, ordained that this act be shared only between husband and wife? He knows that sexual intercourse is much more than a physical act. He knows that it creates more than a oneness in the flesh. It also creates a soul-tie, a bonding in the mind, will, and emotions. It forges between the two participants a spiritual connection.

Who could understand these concepts better than our Heavenly Father who is a Spirit and is Love. When a husband and wife give themselves to each other in the act of making love, the Spirit of God unites their spirits, and they become one. The wife becomes bone of the husband's bone and flesh of the husband's flesh. The spirit of love inspires them with new life in their relationship; and, eventually, they receive, as the fruit of their love, the most wonderful gift of all: a child.

It is a most shameful thing to abuse this wonderful privilege of making love by engaging in it without the blessing of God, our Creator. Since He forged the union of husband and wife and placed sex in the marriage for its protection, when we sin in this way, it is a personal offense to God.

Sin is *disobedience to God,* and when we sin, we are giving the spirit of Satan an opportunity to get involved in our affairs. We are opening a door to him to come in and take control of our lives. That is a most dangerous act.

When someone engages in sexual intercourse out of wedlock, they are out of the will of God. Therefore, it is no longer love making; for God is Love, and He blesses obedience not disobedience. And that which is not blessed of God becomes cursed of Satan.

This is, I believe, why the most offensive, vulgar, nasty, and filthy word in the English language is a curse word used to refer to the act of making love and the reason this has become one of the most frequently used words of profanity.

Could there be a connection between the use of this word and the number of babies born out of wedlock, the number of divorces due to an unfaithful spouses, the number of rapes, the rising occurrences of incest, child molestation, homosexuality, and sexual perversion? I am sure of it.

Could there be a connection between these profane words and the rise in the number of sexually transmitted diseases and their deadliness, or in the dramatic rise in the number of out-of-wedlock and teen pregnancies? I have no doubt about it.

Why do so many of the profane and vulgar curse words have sexual connotations, some even referring crudely to the reproductive organs of the body? Satan hates what God created for good and is determined to degrade it and destroy its beauty. And God will not hold guiltless those who use these curses.

- 9 -

CONDEMNING MEN AND WOMEN TO HELL

The Lord is not slack concerning his promise, as some men count slackness; but is longsuffering to us-ward, not willing that any should perish but that all should come to repentance.

2 Peter 3:9

God is Love and has gone to great extremes to show His love to mankind. The love that He displayed on Calvary is greater than any other. The Scriptures declare:

Greater love hath no man than this, that a man lay down his life for his friends. John 15:13

Jesus Christ is the Son of God. He didn't have to leave Heaven. He didn't have to take off His royal garments. Yet He willingly suffered and died to save us from spending eternity in a burning Hell.

It is only through this, God's plan of salvation through Christ, that any of us has an opportunity to repent of our sins and accept Jesus as our Lord and Savior. This guarantees us the privilege of living forever with Him in peace and joy. What more could we ask?

When we tell someone, therefore, to "go to hell," we are saying that we do not want the love that Jesus has for them to be effective in their lives. We are saying that we don't want them to accept Jesus Christ as their Lord and Savior and to be forgiven for their sins. And when we do this, we are pitting our will directly against the express will of God. He doesn't want anyone to perish:

> *For God so loved the world, that He gave His only begotten Son, that whoever believes in Him should not perish, but have eternal life.*
>
> John 3:16 NAS

When we tell someone to "go to hell," we are judging them and sentencing them to eternal damnation. It is an expression of hate and contempt. Since none of us wants to go to Hell ourselves, we are setting ourselves up as judges of our fellowman when we try to send them there. This is very dangerous because Jesus said:

> *Judge not, that you be not judged. For with what judgement that you judge, you shall be judged.*
>
> Matthew 7:1-2

So, if you don't want to go there yourself, you must

be careful not to wish anyone else were sent there.

What is this Hell to which we are condemning others? The Bible describes it as *"hell fire"* (Matthew 5:22, 18:9), a place of the destruction of *"both soul and body"* (Matthew 10:28), a place of *"damnation"* (Matthew 23:33), a place *"where their worm dieth not, and the fire is not quenched"* (Mark 9:44,46,48). The rich man who died and went there was *"in torments"* (Luke 16:23). Of this terrible place, Jesus said:

> *But the children of the kingdom shall be cast out into outer darkness: there shall be weeping and gnashing of teeth.* Matthew 8:12

This is clearly neither a place that we want to go nor want someone else to go. And sending people there is a sign of the spirit of Satan who wants nothing more than to drag the soul of all men down to these torments.

This is a serious curse that should never cross our lips, and God will not hold guiltless those who insist on using it.

- 10 -

Referring To Bodily Wastes

A good man out of the good treasure of the heart brings forth good things: and an evil man out of the evil treasure brings forth evil things.

Matthew 12:35

Another of the most frequently used profane words is one that refers to bodily waste. It is uttered in moments of pain, fear, trouble, anger and excitement. It is also used in moments of happiness to express what we seem incapable of expressing in any other way. In this way, it has become an all-purpose word. This word seems to just roll off of the tongue of many people at any given moment. And, because it is heard more and more often, it is repeated more and more often. Profanity is contagious.

This word is spoken too many times when other things need to be said. It is used in times of anger – when words of peace should be spoken. It is spoken in times of trouble – when words of comfort should be spoken. It is spoken in times of fear – when words of faith should be spoken. Because words are so powerful, we must use them to help remedy negative situations, not to complicate or perpetuate them.

But profanity has become such a way of life with many people that these vulgar words or phrases are spoken with no regard to their true meaning or their effects on ourselves and others in our society.

Jesus said:

> *O generation of vipers, how can ye, being evil, speak good things? for out of the abundance of the heart the mouth speaketh.*
> *A good man out of the good treasure of the heart bringeth forth good things: and an evil man out of the evil treasure bringeth forth evil things.*
> *But I say unto you, that every idle word that men shall speak, they shall give account thereof in the day of judgment. For by thy words thou shalt be justified, and by thy words thou shalt be condemned.* Matthew 12:34-37

Let us guard our tongues well and not be caught up in the trend to use such vile and tasteless words.

- 11 -

Taking God's Name In Vain

You shall not use or repeat the name of the Lord your God in vain [that is, lightly or frivolously, in false affirmations or profanely]; for The Lord will not hold him guiltless who takes His name in vain. Exodus 20:7 AMPLIFIED

Many popular curses use the Lord's name in vain. This is such a violation of His person that He has explicitly prohibited such speech in the Ten Commandments.

The command to honor the Lord's name was later repeated to those who loved God and wanted to serve Him in the book of Leviticus, the law:

And you shall not swear by My name falsely, neither shall you profane the name of your God, I am the Lord. Leviticus 19:12

This is a serious matter and God will not hold guiltless the man or woman who profanes His holy name.

There are, as we all well know, many other words and phrases that are vulgar and profane. I have chosen to address the ones that I feel are the most vulgar and offensive. Unfortunately, the words that are the most profane, vulgar and offensive are the ones that are the most frequently used these days. This is a shame and a disgrace to our society, one that must be remedied if we are to remain a great nation and a great people, blessed of God.

Part III

What Can We Do?

- 12 -

Be Renewed Within

> *But those things which proceed out of the mouth come forth from the heart; and they defile the man. For out of the heart proceed evil thoughts, murders, adulteries, fornications, thefts, false witness, blasphemies: These are the things which defile a man.* Matthew 15:18-20

Profanity is an evil that originated with Satan and which, after the fall of man, is natural to the unregenerate heart.

The physical heart is *a hollow, muscular organ that by rhythmic contractions and relaxations keeps the blood in circulation throughout the body.* The Greek word for *heart* is *kardia* which is where we get the word *cardiac. Kardia* refers *to the chief organ of physical life.*

The Hebrew word for heart is *leb* and is used figuratively, for *feelings, the will, and the intellect.* It is also used to refer to *the center of something.* The word *heart* is often used in Scripture to refer to *man's mental and moral activity, both the rational and emotional.* The word *heart* is used to describe *the hidden springs of one's personal life*. The *heart* is *the center of the total personality especially with reference to intuition, feelings or emotion.*

The Bible teaches that man's perversion, wickedness and corruption has its roots in the center of his inward life or *the heart*. Therefore, as the physical heart pumps blood through the entire body, the spiritual heart pumps or circulates sin throughout man's entire being.

The heart is the area of Divine influence which contains the hidden man — the real you.

> *The heart is deceitful above all things, and desperately wicked: who can know it? I the Lord search the heart, I try the reigns [mind] even to give every man according to his ways and according to the fruit of his doings.*
>
> Jeremiah 17: 9-10

Jesus also said:

> *O generation of vipers, how can you being evil, speak good things? for out of the abundance of the heart the mouth speaks. A good man out of the good treasure of the heart bringeth forth good things: and an evil man out of the evil treasure [of his heart] bringeth forth evil things. But I say unto you, that every idle [unprofitable, useless] word that men shall speak, they shall give account thereof in the day of judgment. For by thy words thou shall be justified, and by thy*

words thou shall be condemned.

Matthew 12:34-37

Man was created to be an eternal being. His heart was made to last forever, his blood was pure. Pure life was being circulated throughout his whole system continually. When God breathed the breath of life into man's nostrils, man became a living soul. He was designed to live forever, as fresh, as strong, and as healthy as he was the very first moment that God created him.

Adam, by an act of his free will, chose to turn away from the word of God and follow the words of Satan. As a result, Adam was separated from God and became subject to sin and death. He lost his communion with God and his authority over all of creation.

When God called and asked *"Adam where art thou?"*, out of the deceitfulness of his heart, Adam answered:

I heard thy voice,
I was afraid,
I was naked,

and

I hid myself. Genesis 3:10

When God asked Adam if he had eaten the forbidden fruit, Adam blamed his wife; and she, in turn, blamed the serpent. Thus the curse of sin was established in the earth.

But Jesus Christ who is called, in the Scriptures, *"the Last Adam,"* came to our rescue:

> *And The Word was made flesh and dwelt among us, and we beheld his glory, the glory as of the only begotten of the Father, full of grace and truth.* John 1:14

> *For God so loved the world that he gave His only begotten Son, that whosoever believes in Him should not perish, but have everlasting life.*
> John 3:16

By confessing Jesus as Lord, and believing in our heart that God raised Him from the dead, we can be restored to our original position with God. Recognizing that fact, David prayed:

> *Create in me a clean heart, O God; and renew a right spirit within me.* Psalms 51:10

God promised, through the prophets, to give those who sought Him a changed heart:

> *And I will give them one heart, and I will put a new spirit within you; and I will take the stony heart out of their flesh, and will give them a heart of flesh: That they may walk in my statutes, and keep mine ordinances, and do them:*

and they shall be my people, and I will be their God. But as for them whose heart walketh after the heart of their detestable things and their abominations, I will recompense (pay back) their way upon their own heads, saith the Lord God.
Ezekiel 11:19-21

Many other Scripture passages confirm God's willingness to do this miracle:

Wherewithal shall a young man cleanse his way? By taking heed thereto according to thy word. With my whole heart have I sought thee: O let me not wonder from thy commandments. Thy Word have I hid in my heart, that I might not sin against thee. Psalms 119:9-11

Let the words of my mouth, and the meditations of my heart, be acceptable in thy sight, O Lord, my strength and my redeemer. Psalms 19:14

Keep thy heart with all diligence; for out of it are the issues of life. Put away from you a froward [crooked, perverse] mouth, and perverse lips put far from you. Proverbs 4:23-24

The most important step, then, in casting off the habit of profanity is to accept Jesus as our Lord and Savior and be born again. When we do this, His Spirit lives in us, and we no longer do the things we once did. Paul wrote to the early Church:

Therefore if any man be in Christ, he is a new creature: old things are passed away; behold, all things are become new. 2 Corinthians 5:17

If you would like to be freed from a filthy mind and a filthy tongue, ask God to save you today, to make you clean and give you a new heart. He will hear your cry.

When we accept Christ as our personal Savior, our minds are renewed through the miracle of regeneration. We cannot completely yield to the Spirit of God until that process takes place. Paul wrote:

I beseech you therefore, brethren, by the mercies of God, that you present your bodies a living sacrifice, holy acceptable unto God, which is your reasonable service. And be not conformed to this world: but be ye transformed by the renewing of your mind, that you may prove what is that good, and acceptable, and perfect, will of God. Romans 12:1-2

Our minds continue to be renewed day by day as we meditate on the Word of God. Yielding our minds to the Word of God through meditation allows His Word to mold and shape our thinking. He said:

For my thoughts are not your thoughts, neither are your ways my ways, saith the Lord. For as the heavens are higher than the earth, so are my ways higher than your ways, and my thoughts than your thoughts. Isaiah 55:8-9

God's intervention in our minds, by meditation on His Word, brings understanding for daily living. King David wrote:

> *I have more understanding than all my teachers: for thy testimonies are my meditation. I understand more than the ancients [aged ones], because I keep thy precepts.*
> Psalms 119:99-100

> *The entrance of thy words giveth light; it giveth understanding unto the simple.*
> Psalms 119:130

Joshua spoke to the children of Israel:

> *This book of the law shall not depart out of thy mouth; but thou shall meditate therein day and night, that thou may observe to do according to all that is written therein: for then thou shall make thy way prosperous, and then thou shall have good success.* Joshua 1:8

And Paul wrote to the believers of the New Testament Church:

> *Whatsoever things are true, whatsoever things are honest, whatsoever things are just, whatsoever things are pure, whatsoever things are*

lovely, whatsoever things are of good report; if there be any virtue, if there be any praise, think on these things. Philippians 4:8.

Let God begin the renewal of your mind today!

- 13 -

Guard Against the Profanity In Entertainment and Sports

Be sober, be vigilant; because your adversary the devil, as a roaring lion, walketh about, seeking whom he may devour. 1 Peter 5:8

One of the reasons that profanity has become so entrenched in our society is that it is liberally used by many in the entertainment industry and the sports world. This is a shame because entertainment and sports, in and of themselves, are not bad things.

The word *entertain* means:

1) *To agreeably hold the attention of; to divert; to amuse*
2) *To treat as a guest; show hospitality to*
3) *To admit into or hold in the mind; consider*
4) *To maintain or keep up*
5) *To give admittance or reception to; receive.*

The word has two parts: *enter* which means *to go in,*

and *tain* which means *to hold.* Entertainment should be a blessing.

In the United States we have the advantage of selecting from a wide variety of entertainment such as: amusement parks, television, movies, concerts, music videos, albums, CD's, tapes, video games, arcades, parties, theaters, books, museums, zoos, sports, comedy ... and the list goes on and on. Entertainment is one of the biggest industries in the world, bringing in billions of dollars in revenue annually.

Entertainment serves a useful purpose in our lives. Life can become very stressful, and our minds can become so bogged down with *"the cares of this world"* that if we don't take some time out from our daily routines, our cares, and problems and concentrate on something else for a while, we can be overwhelmed by the things we face. It is healthy to have our attention diverted from pressing issues so that we can refresh our minds with enjoyable thoughts and activities. All of us sometimes need a break from depressing issues, disappointments, frustrations and heartaches. And we can turn to entertainment as a sort of refuge, a means of relaxing.

It is very important, however, that we know what we are exposing ourselves to. When you watch a show of some kind, you are opening yourself up to the spirit that permeates that show. First of all, consider the source of the entertainment, its purpose, its message, and whether it is constructive or destructive.

If you are tired or depressed or frustrated or hurting or desperate, you may be very vulnerable to the attack of the Enemy. Learn to recognize his devices.

Even in times of high spirits – when you seek entertainment as a way to celebrate a victory, a great achievement, or a special event – the Enemy would love to burst your bubble, crash your party, and rain on your parade. Be careful not to allow Satan to work on your mind, your will, and your emotions (soul) and, thus, to get a hold on you.

When we listen to profanity, gossip, vulgar jokes, filthy, violent lyrics, gangster rap, perverted television programs, dirty movies or any other source of filth, we are allowing Satan an opportunity to plant seeds in our minds, seeds that will take root in our hearts and affect every part of our being.

> *For out of the heart are the issues of life.*
>
> Proverbs 4:23

If we continue to receive such negative input, we will soon be giving forth the same type of thoughts and damaging the lives of others around us.

Too many forms of popular entertainment divert our attention in the wrong direction. *Divert* means:

1) *To turn aside from a path or course; to deflect*
2) *To draw off to a different course or purpose*
3) *To distract from serious occupation.*

In many cases, Satan knows that he can't get you to

commit some hideous, vulgar, sinful, or criminal act, so what he does is expose you to the spirits of these same acts in a form that is very exciting, comical and entertaining.

Let each of us take a close and honest look at what we allow to entertain us. Just as everything that glitters is not gold, everything that makes us laugh is not funny; everything that sounds good is not pleasant; everything that relaxes us is not edifying.

Have you ever gone on a vacation that was long overdue, and when you returned you were more exhausted then when you left? You got away, but you didn't accomplish your goal. The goal was to relax and refresh your body, mind and spirit; but something happened to keep you from achieving that end. Relaxation, unwinding, is the motive for the participation of a great many people in various forms of entertainment, but the reality of what actually happens is that they become more tense and irritable than they were to begin with, and many times they don't even know it.

There are a great number of modern artists who have been blessed with musical gifts: great composers, musicians and singers. Their music is fantastic, but the lyrics that accompany the music are profane, suggestive, vulgar and offensive. To allow this type of artistic abuse to *enter[go in]tain[hold]* you is foolish and dangerous. Such music is polluted.

There are many brilliant comedians who can really make us laugh, laugh until we practically fall on the floor. They have the God-given ability to take everyday situations and present them in a way that is truly hilarious. Many comedians, however, spike their humor with words that are crude, profane, vulgar, offensive and degrading. To allow this kind of humor to *enter[go in]tain[hold]* us is very dangerous. It grieves the Holy Spirit in us.

God does want us to be happy:

> *A happy heart is good medicine and a cheerful mind works healing, but a broken spirit dries up the bones.* Proverbs 17:22 AMPLIFIED

But we must be fed a wholesome diet. If we eat food that tastes good, but is spoiled, we will get sick and, in some cases, might even die. Sometimes contaminated food doesn't smell bad or taste bad. The same holds true for some forms of entertainment. Laughter is good, but profanity never produces pleasant fruit.

The same principle applies to many television programs, movies, plays, videos and magazines that glamorize illicit sex, violence, vulgarity and crime. They employ people who are physically attractive and, in many instances, exceptionally talented.

Don't be fooled. Talent, art, and creativity all come from God, the Creator; but people who use their gifts for evil purposes have allowed demonic spirits to influence them, spirits of profanity, vulgarity, pornography and lewdness. Their minds are contaminated, infected, and polluted, and they wish to pollute others. The talent God has invested in them has been turned against His purposes.

One day God will demand a return on His investment. One day He will demand that we all give an account of what we have done with the talents and gifts that He graciously loaned to us. That will be a sad day for many.

Have you ever loaned something to a friend, and when you asked for it, it was returned to you broken, dirty, and misused? This is what many of us have done with the talents that God has given to us. And we will surely be called into account.

Let us not be guilty of encouraging singers, musicians, rappers, actors, dancers, writers, and other artists who continue creating and performing in a profane manner. Let us not encourage them in any way. Let us neither buy their products nor pay to see them perform. If we do, we are as guilty as they because we contribute to and reward them for the abuse of their talent. When we spend money for their products, pay to see them, attend their performances, applaud their performances, or support them in any way, we are giving them motivation to continue as they are. And we are sure that vulgarity and profanity do not enhance creativity, they pollute it.

The entertainment industry is driven by the profit motive and will promote whatever sells — no matter who it hurts. The hope for us is that people sell only what we buy. Every radio and television station has a programing department where the selection and scheduling of television shows and songs to be aired is determined. If enough people make a commitment to stop supporting profane artists, things will change.

The rise in the use of profanity in nationally and internationally televised sporting events is especially alarming since exposure to such language affects our children. When children see their sports heroes, those whose talents they greatly admire, acting in a violent way or using profanity, they often come to think that is acceptable behavior. Consciously or subconsciously, they begin to behave the way they've seen or heard their heroes behave.

But all of us are in the public eye, in one way or another, be it locally, nationally or internationally – in our homes, neighborhoods, schools or wherever we happen to be. Someone is watching you, and someone is listening to you. What message are you sending?

Let us all make a commitment today to stop using and encouraging the use of profanity and immoral suggestions. Let us make a commitment not to support any form of entertainment that is polluted with profanity, vulgarity or violence, and which has no redeeming social or spiritual value. Also let us pray for those who have not yet made such a commitment.

> *Be strong in the Lord [be empowered through your union with Him]; draw your strength from Him [that strength which His boundless might provides].*
>
> *Put on God's whole armor [the armor of a heavy-armed soldier which God supplies], that*

you may be able successfully to stand up against [all] the strategies and deceits of the devil.
For we are not wrestling with flesh and blood [contending only with physical opponents], but against the despotisms, against the powers, against [the master spirits who are] the world rulers of this present darkness, against the spirit forces of wickedness in the heavenly [supernatural] sphere.
Therefore put on God's complete armor, that you may be able to resist and stand your ground on the evil day [of danger], and having done all [the crisis demands] to stand [firmly in your place].
Stand therefore [hold your ground], having tightened the belt of truth around your loins and having put on the breastplate of integrity and of moral rectitude and right standing with God.
And having shod your feet in preparation [to face the enemy with the firm footed stability, the promptness, and the readiness produced by the good news] of the Gospel of peace.
Lift up over all the [covering] shield of saving faith, upon which you can quench all the flaming missiles of the wicked [one].
And take the helmet of salvation and the sword that the Spirit wields, which is the Word of God.

Ephesians 6:10-17 AMPLIFIED

- 14 -

Learn To Tame the Tongue

If any man among you seem to be religious, and bridleth not his tongue, but deceiveth his own heart, this man's religion is vain.

James 1:26

Even for those who have become believers in Jesus Christ, taming the tongue is serious business. Surprisingly, this is one of the major themes of the book of James. It is worthwhile for us to examine here a more detailed passage:

For we all stumble in many ways. If anyone does not stumble in what he says, he is a perfect man, able to bridle the whole body as well.
Now if we put the bits into the horses' mouth so that they may obey us, we direct their entire body as well.
Behold, the ships also, though they are so great and are driven by strong winds, are still directed by a very small rudder, wherever the inclination

of the pilot desires.
So also the tongue is a small part of the body, and yet it boasts of great things. Behold, how great a forest is set aflame by such a small fire!
And the tongue is a fire, the very world of iniquity, the tongue is set among our members as that which defiles the entire body, and sets on fire the course of our life, and is set on fire by hell.
For every species of beasts and birds, of reptiles and creatures of the sea, is tamed, and has been tamed by the human race.
But no one can tame the tongue; it is a restless evil and full of deadly poison.
With it we bless our Lord and Father; and with it we curse men, who have been made in the likeness of God;
From the same mouth come both blessing and cursing. My brethren, these things ought not to be this way.
Does a fountain send out from the same opening both fresh and bitter water?
Can a fig tree, my brethren, produce olives, or a vine produce figs? Neither can salt water produce fresh. James 3:2-12 NAS

What is this powerful and important organ called *the tongue*? The *tongue* is *the movable organ in the floor of the mouth*. It *plays an essential role in tasting, eating, drinking, swallowing and speaking*. The tongue *enables man to utter his thoughts, or to speak what is on his mind, and with the aid of the voice, the tongue has the ability to make one's thoughts audible, or heard by others.* The tongue *gives us the ability to send our thoughts, feelings, opinions, beliefs, fears, messages, and information directly to others.* The tongue is man's *primary tool for communication.*

To communicate is *to impart knowledge, to make known, to give to another, to transmit, to share, to give or interchange thoughts.* As we have seen, this is a most important part of our daily lives.

Too often, however, our tongue is in action, and our mind is still. In other words, we speak without thinking, and by the time we realize what we've said, the damage has been done. And when we speak before we think, we often cause ourselves and others much grief. The tongue is so powerful that it must be used with care.

As James wrote to the early church:

> *For we all stumble in many ways. If anyone does not stumble in what he says, he is a perfect man, able to bridle the whole body as well.*
>
> James 3:2 NAS

We all have had the unpleasant experience of saying the wrong thing, or talking to the wrong person, or saying something the wrong way. The tongue has a way of doing its own thing and we suffer the consequences of its action.

James spoke of the ability of putting a small bit in the mouth of a powerful horse and controlling the direction of its massive body. The same, he said, is true of a great ship. Even in the midst of a great and powerful storm at sea, though the winds toss the ship, and the waves beat against the sides of it, the pilot of the vessel is still able to control the direction that ship takes through the very small rudder.

"So also the tongue...," James said. Like the bit in the mouth of a powerful horse, or the rudder on a great ship, the tongue has the amazing ability to control the direction of an entire life, though it is such a small member of our body.

A small spark can set thousands of acres of forest on fire, killing vegetation, wildlife, and people, polluting the air with deadly smoke, and costing the community millions of dollars in damage, loss of property and repair. The same holds true for the tongue.

So the tongue: *"And the tongue is a fire, the very world of iniquity [wickedness]; the tongue is set among our members [in our body] as that which defiles [contaminates] the entire body, and sets on fire the course of our life, and is set on fire by hell."*

Satan knows very well the power of words. When he convinced man to obey his words in the garden, it gave him the opportunity to poison the heart of man and set his tongue on fire. After that mighty fall, it could be said that out of the abundance of man's deceitful, wicked heart, his mouth would speak and verbalize the curse, and communicate it to others and spread it like wildfire.

With this turn of events an unstoppable force was

set in motion: *"Every species of beasts and birds, of reptiles and creatures of the sea, is tamed, and has been tamed by the human race. But no one can tame the tongue; it is a restless evil and full of deadly poison."*

The human tongue has thus become one of Satan's most powerful tools to accomplish his goals of stealing, killing, and destroying. The tongue is poison, and it burns. Like other deadly weapons of chemical warfare, it releases its product (words) into the atmosphere, and its venom affects anyone who comes into contact with it. At times those affects are not felt or seen until days and even years later. But, invariably, the end result is death.

The tongue is totally contradictory: *"With it we bless our Lord and Father, and with it we curse men, who have been made in the likeness of God; from the same mouth come both blessing and cursing."*

As the Native Americans would say, we "speak with forked tongue." One minute we say one thing, and the next minute we say the opposite. This is true because our hearts are deceitful. We deceive ourselves and others by what we say. And sometimes we even believe our own lies.

Ever since man disobeyed God, his heart has been contaminated or polluted; and *"out of the abundance of the heart the mouth speaks"* (Matthew 12:34). This explains why the heart pumps sweet and bitter (contaminated) water (words) through the tongue. Just as salt water cannot produce fresh, neither can an evil or sinful heart produce words of life.

So what are we to do? Again, the first thing we are

to do is accept Jesus Christ into our hearts as our Lord and Savior, and ask Him to create in us a clean heart. Then, once we have been born again, we must allow the Lord to fill us with His precious Holy Spirit, as He did the disciples on the Day of Pentecost (Acts 2:1-4). Our divided tongue will be set on fire from Heaven, and we will speak with new tongues words which the Holy Spirit will utter through us.

After this happens, let the Lord work through you daily to speak words of life, healing, love, and compassion. Let everyone hear you speaking the wonderful words of God. God said of the man who learns to control his tongue:

> *He that has knowledge spares his words: and a man of understanding is of an excellent spirit. Even a fool when he holds his peace, is counted wise: and he that shutteth his lips is esteemed a man of understanding.* Proverbs 17:27-28

The fact that you are born again and filled with the Spirit is not a guarantee that you will never again be tempted to say something wrong. You will. Because Satan uses the power of wrong words to defeat us, he always tries to get us to fall into this error again. But now that you know the truth about profanity, you can make a conscious choice not to use these words again. You must, for God said:

> *I call heaven and earth to record this day against you, that I have set before you life and death,*

blessing and cursing: therefore CHOOSE LIFE, that both you and your seed [children] may live: that you may love the Lord your God, and that you may obey His voice, and that you may cleave unto Him: for He is your life, and the length of your days: that you may dwell in the land which the Lord sware unto your fathers, to Abraham, to Isaac, and to Jacob, to give them.

Deuteronomy 30:19-20

Let us each, this day, by an act of our will, choose:

Love not Lust
Life not Death
Blessing not Cursing
Obedience not Disobedience
Words that heal, not Words that hurt
Words that inspire, not Words that discourage
Words that create, not Words that destroy
Words that build, not Words that tear down
Words of truth , not Words of deception
The Word of God, not the Word of Satan

Let us daily pray with the Psalmist:

Keep back thy servant also from presumptuous sins; let them not have dominion over me: then shall I be upright, and I shall be innocent from the great transgression. Let the words of my mouth, and the meditations of my heart, be ac-

> *ceptable in thy sight, O Lord, my strength, and my redeemer.* Psalms 19:13-14

Father,

We pray this in the name of Jesus Christ, our Savior.

Amen!

- 15 -

The Conclusion

I have attempted to address a very sensitive issue in a way that would not be crude, improper or offensive. In our society, profanity has become so prevalent and has such a negative effect on all of us, that someone has to make an effort to end it or, at the very least, lessen its use among both our adults and children. My intention was to reveal the true meanings of the most profane words and the damaging effects they have on us, as individuals and on society as a whole. I believe that:

If we change the way we think,
We will change what we say.
If we change what we say,
We will change what we do;
And if we change what we do,
We will change our world.

It is time to make that change.

Jesus Christ is the Word of God, and He came so that we could have life, and have it more abundantly. It is through believing in Him, and receiving and obeying His word (the Holy Bible) that we can change our thoughts to His thoughts and our ways to His ways.

Paul wrote to the Romans:

> *Be not conformed to this world: but be ye transformed by the renewing of your mind, that ye may prove what is that good, and acceptable, and perfect, will of God.* Romans 12:2

I pray that something has been said here to bless you and to encourage you to speak words of life, and not words of death; words of faith and not words of fear; words that build up, and not words that tear down; the Word of God and not words of Satan.

I leave you with these challenging words from the Holy Bible:

> *Let no foul or polluting language, nor evil word nor unwholesome or worthless talk [ever] come out of your mouth, but only such [speech] as is good and beneficial to the spiritual progress of others, as is fitting to the need and the occasion, that it may be a blessing and give grace (God's favor) to those who hear it.*

> *And do not grieve the Holy Spirit of God [do not offend or vex or sadden Him], by whom you*

were sealed (marked, branded as God's own, secured) for the day of redemption (of final deliverance through Christ from evil and the consequences of sin).

Let all bitterness and indignation and wrath (passion, rage bad temper) and resentment (anger, animosity) and quarreling (brawling, clamor, contention) and slander (evil-speaking, abusive or blasphemous language) be banished from you, with all malice (spite, ill will, or baseness of any kind).

And become useful and helpful and kind to one another, tenderhearted (compassionate, understanding, loving-hearted), forgiving one another [readily and freely], as God in Christ forgave you.

Ephesians 4:29-32 AMPLIFIED

Amen!

SURRETT MINISTRIES includes the following outreaches:

- **Men In the Hood** — This ministry reaches out to men of all ages who are bound by drugs, gangs and incarceration.
- **The Josiah Generation** — This ministry is committed to a revival among young people between the ages of 11 and 19.
- **Kingdom Kids** — This ministry is to children, from preschool to 10 years old.
- **H.E.R.O.** — This ministry (Health, Education, and Respect for Oneself and Others) teaches self-esteem and drug prevention.

For additional information, or to receive audio tapes, write or call:

Surrett Ministries

P.O. 6719
Chicago, IL 60680-6719
(708) 333-0527